LEADING THE WAY TO JESUS

Transformed
CHRISTIANS

Natasha Reid

Transformed Christians
Leading the Way to Jesus

NATASHA REID
reid4god@gmail.com

ISBN: 978-1-943342-27-3

Printed in the USA.
All rights reserved

Published by: Destined To Publish | Flossmoor, Illinois
www.DestinedToPublish.com

ACKNOWLEDGMENT

I thank God for birthing the vision and idea in me to write this book. I have prayed to God and listened to Him for instructions in writing this book, and He has given me wisdom, direction, and guidance.

Thank you to my Pastors, Bishops James and Grace Blue, who are my spiritual role models and mentors. They have helped to mold and shape me to be the woman of God that I am today. I learned about biblical and spiritual principles from them. They have equipped me for greatness as a Christian and in ministry. I give special thanks to Bishop Grace Blue, who is an author herself. She encouraged me to write this book and has prayed for me during the writing process. She agreed to be a reader for my manuscript and offered some helpful suggestions for me. Also, she agreed to write a foreword for me, which I appreciate.

Thank you to Minister Veronica Bea, who is also an author. She played a role in encouraging me to write this book, and I consider her to be one of my Spiritual Mentors, because she has always been an inspiration and encouragement to me. Minister Veronica Bea helps to impart biblical and spiritual principles to me as I listen and learn from her spiritual preaching and teaching. I have had opportunities to be on Prayer Lines with her, have Spiritual Fellowship with her, and so on. She has helped to equip me for greatness.

Thanks to my mother, Valrie J. Reid, who encouraged me in writing this book. She is an awesome prayer intercessor and woman of faith. She is a very compassionate person who supports me in achieving my goals.

FOREWORD

Being a Christian for most of my life and a Pastor for close to 40 years, I've seen a lot of faces, been to a lot of places, and wondered why many people who have received salvation through the saving grace of Jesus Christ and profess their love of God are content to stay the same way they were before they came to Christ. Too many do not realize that their life needs to be a reflection of the Christ inside.

I've had the pleasure and honor, along with my husband, of being one of Natasha's Pastors for over 15 years and have witnessed her growth in the Lord. She's always been one that took her Christian walk seriously, going from one who was not as confident in who she is to one who confidently expounds the Word of God in power and in might! In fact, she is one of our licensed ministers in the area of Evangelism, and she is certainly a prayer warrior! Natasha is a true blessing to the Body of Christ and to our church, Cincinnati Bible Way.

This book that Natasha Reid has written, Transformed Christians: Leading the Way to Jesus, is a must read and an answer for those that are not content with just being saved but want to be, as Romans 12:1;2 says, transformed by becoming more like our Savior Jesus Christ, getting rid of the old sinful nature and now walking in the renewed, transformed, righteous mind of Jesus Christ!

What Natasha is shedding light on in her book is a life that she's living. A transformed life! She makes it clear that it's about much more than speaking and sharing the Word of God to others: more importantly, it's about being an epistle, a life that is read or viewed by others in becoming more like Christ. People respond more to what they see us do rather than what they hear us say.

In her book, Natasha focuses in on the necessity of living a life that is pleasing to God and obedient to His Word. She takes the time to share her journey in living a transformed life so that those that read will not only see that it is beneficial but also know that it is doable. She reiterates the fact that holiness is a lifestyle that all Believers in Jesus Christ should want to strive toward. Holiness should be the standard of practice for all Believers because we love our Father God and want to be pleasing in His sight!

Natasha gives practical keys to how to live a transformed life, as well as what ingredients need to be in the life of a Transformed Believer in Jesus Christ. She also has prayers for each area based on biblical principles of living a transformed life to assist the reader in their prayer life.

According to Natasha, living a transformed life will allow us to more effectively lead others to Jesus, to salvation, because they will see the Christ in us more clearly! It's not enough to say we are Christians, but they will know that we are Christians by the transformed lives we lead as we lead them to Jesus!

Blessings,
Apostle Grace M. Blue

CONTENT

INTRODUCTION

One of the main reasons people say they don't go to church is because "there are too many hypocrites in church." Christians are to be authentically transformed. It is only when Christians are transformed that they can authentically be representatives for Christ Jesus.

God desires for everyone to be saved. Initially, being saved is simply inviting Jesus into your heart and making that confession that He is your Lord and Savior. But salvation is a continual process. In fact, salvation involves going through the process of transformation and being born again by the Holy Spirit. These topics and more are covered in Chapter 1.

Before Jesus was crucified, died on the cross, and rose from the dead in three days, He told His disciples about how God will send the Holy Spirit to be our Advocate and to teach us. Chapter 2 discusses how, as a result, Christians are to be led by the Holy Spirit and should submit to the Spirit's leading, guidance, and direction of the Holy Spirit.

As Christians continue going through the transformation process, it's important to deny the flesh and the works of the flesh. This will allow us to be pleasing in God's sight. There are good Scripture references and illustrations on how to do this in Chapter 3.

Character and integrity are very important. There are many Scriptures that illustrate to us Christians how to be Holy and live a lifestyle of holiness. One avenue for Christians to display being Holy and have character and integrity is to be obedient to God's Word and to display the fruits of the Spirit, which the Holy Spirit produces in our lives. This is covered in detail in Chapter 4.

Chapter 5 illustrates that our Lord and Savior Jesus was and still is our ultimate example on how to walk in our authority in living as Christians. Jesus was perfect and never sinned. He was totally obedient to God. He displayed many signs, wonders, and miracles, and He healed and delivered many people. Therefore, for us as Christians, wouldn't it be a good idea to be an imitator of Jesus?

When Christians are authentically transformed, they can be the bridge to draw the unsaved to salvation in Jesus. Christians should be able to be effective witnesses for Jesus to those who are unsaved. These topics and more are covered in Chapter 6, along with a salvation prayer for those who are not yet saved or for Christians to lead others to salvation.

Another aspect of being authentically transformed is having an open communication (prayer life) with God. Prayer is simply expressing your cares and concerns to God. There are many different types of prayers, including intercession prayers for others, salvation prayers, repentant prayers, and prayer requests to God for personal needs. It is important for Christians to develop a prayer life with God. Think of prayer as just talking to God about the concerns that are on your heart. As Christians pray to God, it helps us to develop an intimate relationship with Him, and it helps us to activate our faith.

I have included prayers in this book based on the biblical principles that are described throughout the chapters. As I describe different biblical truths and principles in this book, the prayers within each chapter act as an impartation of the biblical principles into your spirit. The prayers are written in a format for the reader to pray these biblical truths into their lives. It's one thing to read about these biblical principles, but it's another level to pray for them to be activated in your life. There are five additional prayers at the end of the book that give guidance for New Christians. New Christians need direction and guidance from God through a seasoned Christian to enable them to be discipled into spiritual maturity. The five additional prayers at the end of the book provide encouragement and edification for New Christians along with Scriptures for them to meditate on. In addition, I have pages reserved for you to write your own personal prayers unto God.

As you read this book, allow it to minister to you, encourage you, and give you applications for your spiritual walk in Christ.

Chapter 1

TRANSFORMED FROM GLORY TO GLORY

Toward the end of the year 2021, God birthed the passion in me to write this book. When I think about it, this book is a result of my experiences of being a Christian and attending church services, things that may have bothered me over the years of my Christian experience, my experiences in ministry, and my passion to minister and be a blessing to others.

I have had many ministry and leadership opportunities at my current church, which is Cincinnati Bible Way Church. I had the opportunity to be the Ministry Leader over the Health Ministry at my church for seven years before it was time for me to pass the baton to someone else. Currently, I have been the Ministry Leader over the "Good Samaritans" Outreach Ministry at my church for nine years. In addition, I have been through three years of Ministry Training at my church. In 2017, I received my Ministry License to preach and teach the Word of God.

In this chapter, I will be describing how Christians need to be transformed. The Greek word for "transform" is *metamorphoo*, which means a change of condition, or to form. In other words, "transform" means to change one's form. The Greek meaning of the word "transform" is used in both **2 Corinthians 3:18** and **Romans**

12:2, and both Scriptures illustrate that Christians are to be transformed in mind and heart.

In the **New King James Version**, **2 Corinthians 3:18** says, *"But we all, with unveiled face, beholding as in a mirror the glory of the Lord, are being transformed into the same image from glory to glory, just as by the Spirit of the Lord."* The theme of this verse is that Christians are being transformed into the image of the Lord. Amen.

Sometimes it's good to look at different translations of a Scripture, so now I want to give the same verse in another translation that I personally love, **The Passion Translation (TPT):** *"We can all draw close to him with the veil removed from our faces. And with no veil we all become like mirrors who brightly reflect the glory of the Lord Jesus. We are being transfigured into his very image as we move from one brighter level of glory to another. And this glorious transfiguration comes from the Lord, who is the Spirit."*

Personally, I am amazed at how God has transformed my life over the years since I have been saved. He has transformed my prayer life, and I am now a member of the prayer team at Cincinnati Bible Way Church. Also, God has transformed, molded, and shaped me with leadership abilities, and I have had opportunities to lead multiple ministries at my church.

It is necessary for us to accept Jesus into our heart for salvation, but there's more to it than that: salvation is a continual process. God wants to continually mold and shape us into His image.

Let's consider the beginning of time when God created the heavens and the earth, specifically when God created the first man and woman on earth, Adam and Eve. The Scripture **Genesis 1:26a (NLT)** is illustrated like this: *"Then God said, 'Let us make human beings in our image to be like us.'"* **Genesis 1:27 (NLT)** then says, *"So God created human beings in his own image. In the image of God he created them; male and female he created them."*

The key words in these verses tell us that God made human beings in His own image. Why would God want us human beings to be created in His image? One reason that God created us in His image is because He is Holy, and He wants us to be Holy and live a lifestyle of Holiness. This is illustrated in **1 Peter 1:14-16 (NLT)**, which says, *"So you must live as God's obedient children. Don't slip back into your old ways of living to satisfy your own desires. You didn't know any better then. But now you must be holy in everything you do, just as God who chose you is holy. For the Scriptures say, 'You must be holy because I am holy.'"*

Personally, I am committed to living a lifestyle of Holiness. For instance, there are some activities that I simply will not do or have quit doing, as I strive more and more to be spiritually mature in the Lord. For example, I choose not to go to night clubs to have fun. Of course, all of us want to be able to have fun at times, whether you're a Christian or not. However, as Christians, we should not be doing every activity that those who are not yet saved are doing. If we as Christians continue to do the same activities as those who are not yet saved, then they may think of us as hypocrites and even be bold enough to tell us so. (Amen—or ouch!) Let's just keep it real.

The Scripture **1 Peter 4:3-4 (TPT)** challenges all of us Christians to live a lifestyle of Holiness, as it states, *"For you have already spent enough time doing what unbelievers love to do—living in debauchery, sensuality, partying, drunkenness, wild drinking parties, and the worship of demons. They marvel that you no longer rush to join them in the excesses of their corrupt lifestyles, and so they vilify you."*

Personally, at times, I have had some of my friends say to me that "I can't do or say this around you because I know that you're a Christian," or "I know that you're a good person." I allow my lifestyle to be a witness. I will discuss more about allowing your lifestyle to be a witness in a later chapter. The point is, people should be able to see and discern the Christ Jesus in us, and we should also be examples for others as Christians.

Another reason that God created us in His image is because God despises sin, and unfortunately, we are sinners. A Scripture that illustrates how God despises sin is **1 John 3:9 (NLT)**: *"Those who have been born into God's family do not make a practice of sinning, because God's life is in them. So they can't keep on sinning, because they are children of God."* Usually, the Holy Spirit will convict us when we are in the midst of committing a sin. As a result, because we want to be pleasing in God's sight, we should repent and turn away from sin.

As Christians, we should discipline ourselves to turn away from sin. The Scripture **Hebrews 12:1 (NLT)** illustrates how to turn away from sin: *"Therefore, since we are surrounded by such a huge crowd of witnesses to the life of faith, let us strip off every weight that slows us down, especially the sin that so easily trips us up. And let us run with endurance the race God has set before us."*

In addition, Christians must be rebirthed by the Holy Spirit, better known as being born again. A good biblical illustration of what it means to be born again is in **John 3:1-8 (NLT)**. Specifically, **John 3:3 (NLT)** states, "Jesus replied, *'I tell you the truth, unless you are born again, you cannot see the Kingdom of God.'"* Then, in **John 3:6 k(NLT)**, Jesus says, *"Humans can reproduce only human life, but the Holy Spirit gives birth to spiritual life."*

Personally, I have been saved since 1993, but it wasn't until the year 2001 that the transformation process into spiritual growth significantly started in me. At that time, I began to learn the Scriptures more in depth with an increased hunger for them. God started to impart more spiritual understanding to me, and my relationship with God started to grow deeper. In 2001, I joined an Equipping Ministry, which was where I learned how to speak in tongues. As a matter of fact, speaking in tongues is one of the manifestations of being born again. That same year, I also learned about the Fivefold Ministry Gifts of Apostles, Prophets, Evangelists, Pastors, and Teachers from **Ephesians 4:11-13 (NLT)**. While I was a part of the Equipping Ministry, it was often preached and taught to us to live a lifestyle of Holiness and to turn away from sinful lifestyles. I had been saved for eight years before I started my transformation process of no longer conforming to the customs of the world or my former lifestyle of how I was before I got saved.

It's important to note that being saved does not mean that you are automatically transformed as a New Christian. In fact, being saved is simply believing in your heart that Jesus rose from the dead and confessing with your mouth that Jesus is your Savior, as illustrated in **Romans 10:9-10 (NLT)**. However, being transformed means that you are no longer a participant in a sinful lifestyle.

As Christians, we should submit ourselves to God for Him to mold and shape us or transform us to be pleasing in His sight. The Scripture **Romans 12:2 (NLT)** says, *"Don't copy the behavior and customs of this world, but let God transform you into a new person by changing the way you think. Then you will learn to know God's will for you, which is good and pleasing and perfect."*

Prayer: God, my prayer is that you will continue your transforming work in us. Yes, God, we submit and surrender ourselves to you. We humble ourselves before you. We allow you, God, to mold and shape us. God, we want to be pleasing in your sight. In Jesus' Name, Amen.

Write Your Own Prayer

LED BY THE HOLY SPIRIT

Christians are to be led by the Holy Spirit. The Holy Spirit is our Advocate. This is revealed in the biblical words of our Savior Jesus Christ as illustrated in the Scripture of **John 14:16-17a (NLT)**, which says, *"And I will ask the Father, and he will give you another Advocate, who will never leave you. He is the Holy Spirit, who leads into all truth."* Another Scripture that reveals that the Holy Spirit is our Advocate through the spoken words of Jesus is **John 14:26 (NLT)**, which says, *"But when the Father sends the Advocate as my representative—that is, the Holy Spirit—he will teach you everything and will remind you of everything I have told you."* In addition, in **John 16 (NLT)**, Jesus teaches us more details about how the Holy Spirit advocates for us. Specifically, in **John 16:7-8 (NLT)**, Jesus says, *"But in fact, it is best for you that I go away, because if I don't, the Advocate won't come. If I do go away, then I will send him to you. And when he comes, he will convict the world of its sin, and of God's righteousness, and of the coming judgment."*

Another way that the Holy Spirit advocates for us is by Intercession of Prayer on our behalf. This is illustrated through the Scripture **Romans 8:26-27 (NLT)**, which says, *"And the Holy Spirit helps us* *in our weakness. For example, we don't know what God wants us to pray for. But the Holy Spirit prays for us with groanings that cannot be expressed in words. And the Father who knows all hearts knows what the Spirit is saying, for the Spirit pleads for us believers in harmony with God's own will."* When Christians speak in tongues, it is the Holy Spirit that is praying through them directly to God as an Advocate. Two illustrations of this in Scripture are in **1 Corinthians 14:14a (NLT)**, which says, *"For if I pray in tongues, my spirit is praying,"* and **1 Corinthians 14:2 (NLT)**, which says, *"For if you have the ability to speak in tongues, you will be talking only to God, since people won't be able to understand you. You will be speaking by the power of the Spirit, but it will all be mysterious."* Personally, I try to speak in tongues as much as I can throughout the day, such as when I'm driving in my car, while doing house chores, and during my devotional times with God. It is a heavenly privilege for Christians to be able to have the Holy Spirit to advocate for us.

Prayer: Heavenly God, thank you for sending the Holy Spirit to be our Advocate. Please help us to submit and surrender to the Holy Spirit as it convicts us of our sins and reveals righteousness to us. God, help us to submit ourselves to the Holy Spirit for Intercession of Prayer. Heavenly God, for those who do not yet speak in tongues, I pray that you will baptize them in the Spirit with the evidence of speaking in tongues. Also, God, for those of us who do already speak in tongues, please help us to develop the spiritual discipline to speak in tongues daily. In Jesus' Name, Amen.

In addition, the Holy Spirit will teach us. As a matter of fact, I just got reminded by the Holy Spirit about a personal testimony that I have about when the Holy Spirit has taught me. I am a licensed practical nurse (LPN) by occupation. One time when I was in nursing school,

I had to drive 45 minutes to a nursing clinical site in an area of town that I was not familiar with. I would have to use my GPS to get there, and again to get back home. One morning when I was on my way to this nursing clinical site, my GPS was not working to guide me to get there. Let me tell you, I had to depend on the Holy Spirit to get me to the site. The Holy Spirit reminded me of the exact route that I took to get there; the whole 45-minute drive that morning was all led by the Holy Spirit, and I arrived safely without the GPS. Now, for this 45-minute drive to the nursing clinical site, I had to take at least two or three highways to get there, and it was in an unfamiliar area of town. Let me testify, only the Holy Spirit could have gotten me there safely without using the GPS.

The Holy Spirit will teach us. This is illustrated in the Scripture **1 John 2:27 (NLT)**, which says, *"But you have received the Holy Spirit, and he lives within you, so you don't need anyone to teach you what is true. For the Spirit teaches you everything you need to know, and what he teaches is true—it is not a lie. So just as he has taught you, remain in fellowship with Christ."*

The Holy Spirit guides us. Personally, I try to make it a daily practice to say this prayer to myself: "Holy Spirit, please lead, guide, and direct me." I train myself to be sensitive to the promptings of the Holy Spirit as often as possible. For example, one way that I try to practice being guided by the Holy Spirit is that when I am indecisive about what to do in a particular situation, I may pray, "Holy Spirit, what should I do?"

One Scripture reference about the Holy Spirit guiding us is in **Romans 8:14 (NLT)**, which says, *"For all who are led by the Spirit of God are children of God."* Another one comes from **Galatians 5:25 (NLT)**, which says, *"Since we are living by the Spirit, let us follow the Spirit's leading in every part of our lives."*

It is a privilege having the Holy Spirit as our Advocate to teach us, lead us, and guide us. I encourage you to try to make it a daily practice to commune with the Holy Spirit.

Prayer: Heavenly God, please help us to be humble enough to allow the Holy Spirit to teach us. God, I pray that you also help us to allow the Holy Spirit to guide us. Yes, Holy Spirit, please lead, guide, and direct us. Heavenly God, please help us to be sensitive to the promptings of the Holy Spirit. Also, God, my prayer is that you help us to follow the Spirit's leading in every part of our lives. In Jesus' Name, Amen.

Write Your Own Prayer

_____

_____

_____

_____

_____

_____

_____

_____

_____

_____

_____

_____

_____

_____

_____

_____

_____

_____

Chapter 3

DENY THE FLESH

Christians are to deny the flesh and the works of the flesh in order to be pleasing in God's sight. When Christians deny the flesh, they don't let sin control the way they live.

A Scripture reference related to the biblical topic of denying the flesh is in **Ephesians 4:22-24 (NLT)**, which says, "*Throw off your old sinful nature and your former way of life, which is corrupted by lust and deception. Instead, let the Spirit renew your thoughts and attitudes. Put on your new nature created to be like God—truly righteous and holy.*"

Every now and then, it is good to assess our growth. Ask yourself, how have I matured or grown up over the past five years? I am writing this in 2022, and personally, I believe that I have changed and matured some since 2017. In the past five years, I graduated from nursing school and became an LPN, and I also received my Ministry License. In terms of how I have changed and matured spiritually since 2017, I believe that I have developed a deeper understanding of the Bible. Literally, the Scriptures have become more unveiled and easier for me to understand. This has transformed me spiritually, because I have matured in my understanding of the Scriptures and received deeper revelations and spiritual insights.

In the past five years, I also started taking Evangelism Ministry Classes, and the evangelist anointing on my life is now stronger and more developed. I have been transformed into a deeper manifestation of evangelizing to people. My transformation process of coming into the manifestation of my evangelist anointing has led me into two main avenues of evangelism. First, I have been transformed into more spiritual boldness to evangelize to homeless people on the streets. Initially, I meet the practical needs of homeless people by lending them money, and then I meet their spiritual needs by giving them a Bible tract and/or asking them, "Are you saved?" Secondly, my transformation process into a stronger and more developed evangelist anointing has led me to start giving the Call to Salvation at my church toward the end of the service. This gives the opportunity for salvation to people who watch our church service online and are not yet saved. Also, over the past five years since 2017, I have started preaching and teaching the Word of God on Facebook Live. These are just some of the ways that I have changed and matured over the past five years. It is a good idea for all of us to spiritually assess our spiritual growth every now and then over the years.

In addition, denying the flesh also means resisting sinful desires. The Scripture **Galatians 5:19-21a (NLT)** says, *"When you follow the desires of your sinful nature, the results are very clear: sexual immorality, impurity, lustful pleasures, idolatry, sorcery, hostility, quarreling, jealousy, outbursts of anger, selfish ambition, dissension, division, envy, drunkenness, wild parties, and other sins like these."* Also, **Galatians 5:24 (NLT)** says, *"Those who belong to Christ Jesus have nailed the passions and desires of their sinful nature to his cross and crucified them there."*

Prayer: Heavenly God, please help us to throw off our old sinful nature. Yes, God, please help us not to allow sin to control the way we live. God, I ask that you renew our thoughts and attitudes in a way that will be pleasing in your sight, based on the Scripture **(Ephesians 4:22-24, NLT).** Oh God, let the words of our mouth and the meditation of our heart be acceptable in your sight **(Psalm 19:14, KJV)**. Heavenly God, please give us the strength to resist sinful desires. In Jesus' Name, Amen.

One way to deny the flesh and resist sinful desires is to be careful what you allow to enter your mind, your eye gate, and your ear gate, and what you allow to come out of your mouth. Let me give you some illustrations. First, be careful what you allow to enter your mind. When bad thoughts come into our mind, we are to cast them down, just as the Scripture says in **2 Corinthians 10:5 (KJV)**: *"Casting down imaginations, and every high thing that exalteth itself against the knowledge of God, and bringing into captivity every thought to the obedience of Christ."* It's very important not to let bad thoughts stay in our mind.

In addition, we should be careful what we allow to enter our eye gate. In other words, watch what you allow your eyes to see. One example I can give is that you should not allow yourself to sin by watching pornography videos. Watching pornography videos could cause you to fall into the sin of lust. Therefore, it is good to deny the flesh by not allowing your eyes to watch these videos.

Also, we should be careful what we allow to enter our ear gate—what we allow our ears to listen to. My personal testimony is that I stopped listening to secular music years ago. I am not saying that listening to secular music is a sin; however, I have personally chosen not to listen to it anymore and to listen mainly to worship music. Personally, for me, an avenue to deny my flesh is not to listen to music with curse words or sexually explicit lyrics.

We should also be careful about the words we allow to come out of our mouth. For example, the Scriptures tell us not to misuse God's name. The biblical reference is **Exodus 20:7a (NLT)**, which says, *"You must not misuse the name of the Lord your God."* For example, if someone were to say "Oh my God" while angry, they may not realize it, but that is a form of misusing God's name. It is very important for us to be careful of our speech as an avenue to deny our flesh.

Prayer: Heavenly God, please help us to be careful of what we allow to enter our minds. Yes, God, if bad thoughts come into our minds that we discern are not from you, please help us to rebuke all bad and negative thoughts. Also, God, I pray that you will help us to be careful about what we allow our eyes to see. Holy God, please give us the discernment not to watch any TV shows or movies that have content in them that is against your will. Likewise, God, please help us to the best of our ability to be careful about what we allow our ears to hear. Heavenly God, please help us to be careful of our speech. God, I pray the Scripture of **Psalm 141:3 (NLT)** into our lives. Yes, God, take control of what we say and guard our lips. In Jesus' Name, Amen.

Another avenue for Christians to deny their flesh is to daily repent of their sins. One Scripture illustration of this is **1 John 1:9 (TPT)**, which says, *"But if we freely admit our sins when his light uncovers them, he will be faithful to forgive us every time. God is just to forgive us our sins because of Christ, and he will continue to cleanse us from all unrighteousness."*

To avoid allowing sin to take root in your life, it is good to repent from your sins immediately or as soon as possible. Repenting daily and quickly from our sins is an avenue to keep ourselves pure and pleasing in God's sight. In addition, if we have done any sins toward other people or have offended others, we must repent of those sins. Forgiveness is also very important. When you forgive people of their offenses toward you, it delivers you, and it is for your benefit.

Another good Scripture reference about repentance is **Acts 3:19-21 (NLT)**, which says, *"Now repent of your sins and turn to God, so that your sins may be wiped away. Then times of refreshment will come from the presence of the Lord, and he will again send you Jesus, your appointed Messiah. For he must remain in heaven until the time for the final restoration of all things, as God promised long ago through his holy Prophets."*

The entire chapter of **Psalm 51** gives us a good Scripture illustration and biblical example of a prayer of repentance to God. This Scripture is an actual prayer of repentance from the biblical character David to God as he repented for his sin of adultery. We as Christians can also pray or use this psalm as a model of a prayer of repentance to God. Personally, I like to use some verses from **Psalm 51** when I am repenting of my sins to God. Specifically, we can pray **Psalm 51:10 (TPT)**, which says, *"Keep creating in me a clean heart. Fill me with pure thoughts and holy desires, ready to please you."*

Fasting is another avenue to denying the flesh. Vine's Expository Dictionary has a few definitions for fasting: a voluntary abstinence from food, not eating, a lack of food or abstaining from eating. There are different types of fasts. One type is an absolute fast, in which people abstain from eating food for a couple of days. Another type of fast is a liquid or juice fast, where people usually just drink water and/or fruit and vegetable juice. The Daniel Fast is a type of fast where people eat only fruit and vegetables while drinking only water and fruit and vegetable juice.

When you decide to fast, you will need to determine how many days you will be fasting for, such as one, three, seven, 21, or 40 days. However, it is totally between you and God what type of fast you choose to do and for how many days. The main thing is that fasting is an avenue to deny your flesh and get closer and more intimate with God.

Before I go on any further, let me mention now that while you are fasting, prayer is essential. In fact, fasting and praying are to be done together, as Jesus stated in the Scriptures. For example, in **Matthew 17:21 (NKJV)**, Jesus tells His disciples, *"However, this kind does not go out except by prayer and fasting."*

There are many reasons to deny the flesh through fasting and praying, and it has many benefits. First, when we fast and pray, we allow ourselves to be more in tune with the Holy Spirit. It allows us to develop more intimacy with God, because we are denying the flesh and removing worldly distractions. When we fast and pray, it also allows us to receive great revelations from God, because we will be more in tune with God to hear from Him. Furthermore, healing and deliverance can take place during fasting and praying. It is healthy for us to fast, and when we pray as well, we tear down strongholds. Also, fasting and praying brings a breakthrough for whatever we are believing God to do for us on our behalf.

To write this book, I did 21 days of fasting and praying for my breakthrough and revelations from God and the Holy Spirit. Whenever I am seeking revelation from God or am in need for a breakthrough,

I will just fast and pray. I usually do the Daniel Fast, which consists of mainly fruits and vegetables and drinking water, fruit juice, and vegetable juice. When I fast, I determine how many days I will be fasting for. I also write down a list of Scriptures that I will be meditating on that relate to the reason why I have decided to fast.

Prayer: Heavenly God, please help us to deny the flesh and the works of the flesh in order to be pleasing in your sight. God, I ask for your strength to help us resist sinful desires. Father God, please convict us to daily and quickly repent of our sins. Also, God, please help us to forgive others who have offended us in any way quickly, just as you have forgiven us of our sins. Furthermore, God, I ask that you would have us be disciplined enough to spiritually assess ourselves every now and then. Heavenly God, I pray the prayer of **Psalm 51:10**: yes, God, create in us a clean heart, fill us with pure thoughts and Holy desires. In Jesus' Name, Amen.

Write Your Own Prayer

_____

_____

_____

_____

_____

_____

_____

_____

_____

_____

_____

_____

_____

_____

_____

Chapter 4

FRUITS OF THE SPIRIT

Christians should have character and integrity. Nobody is perfect except for our Lord and Savior Jesus Christ, but the Scriptures tell us in **1 Peter 1:16** to be Holy because God is Holy. A good Scripture reference comes from **Ephesians 5:9-10 (KJV)**, which says, *"For the fruit of the Spirit is in all goodness and righteousness and truth; proving what is acceptable unto the Lord."*

Matthew 7:15-20 has a good biblical illustration of Jesus teaching about fruit in people's lives. Specifically, **Matthew 7:15-16a (NLT)** says, *"Beware of false prophets who come disguised as harmless sheep but are really vicious wolves. You can identify them by their fruit, that is, by the way they act."* **Matthew 7:17-18 (NLT)** says, *"A good tree produces good fruit, and a bad tree produces bad fruit. A good tree can't produce bad fruit, and a bad tree can't produce good fruit."* **Matthew 7:20 (NLT)** says, *"Yes, just as you can identify a tree by its fruit, so you can identify people by their actions."*

In addition, **Galatians 5:22-23 (NLT)** lists nine Fruits of the Spirit that we as Christians are to display: *"But the Holy Spirit produces this kind of fruit in our lives: love, joy, peace, patience, kindness, goodness, faithfulness, gentleness, and self-control. There is no law against these things!"*

The first Fruit of the Spirit listed is love. It's no wonder, because God is love, and since we are created in God's image, we are also to display love. A good Scripture reference is **1 John 4:16-17a (NLT)**, which says, *"We know how much God loves us, and we have put our trust in his love. God is love, and all who live in love live in God, and God lives in them. And as we live in God, our love grows more perfect."*

Another good Scripture reference about love comes from **John 13:35 (NLT)**, in which Jesus says, *"Your love for one another will prove to the world that you are my disciples."*

Furthermore, in **Luke 6:27 (NLT)**, Jesus says, *"But to you who are willing to listen, I say, love your enemies! Do good to those who hate you."* He continues in **Luke 6:35-36 (NLT)**: *"Love your enemies! Do good to them. Lend to them without expecting to be repaid. Then your reward from heaven will be very great, and you will truly be acting as children of the Most High, for he is kind to those who are unthankful and wicked. You must be compassionate, just as your Father is compassionate."*

Personally, I must admit that at times, it feels hard for me to love my enemies. However, over the years, I have learned some constructive ways to do this. I once had a mentor who told me, "There are some people that you have to love from a distance." I have found this advice to be true, because you can love some people as much as possible, but sadly, they refuse to love you. Another way that I have learned to love my enemies is by praying for them. When you do this, you are to follow the leading of the Holy Spirit on how to pray blessings over your enemies. A good Scripture reference regarding praying for your enemies is **Matthew 5:44-45a (NLT)**, which says, *"But I say, love your enemies! Pray for those who persecute you! In that way, you will be acting as true children of your Father in heaven."*

The second Fruit of the Spirit listed in **Galatians 5** is joy. One good Scripture about the fruit of joy comes from **Psalm 16:11 (TPT)**: *"Because of you, I know the path of life, as I taste the fullness of joy in your presence. At your right side I experience divine pleasures forevermore!"* Another one comes from **Philippians 4:4 (NLT)**: *"Always be full of joy in the Lord. I say it again—rejoice!"* Likewise, **Nehemiah 8:10b (NLT)** says, *"The joy of the Lord is your strength"*

Personally, I can testify to how the joy of the Lord is my strength. Praise and worship has been a manifestation of the joy of the Lord being my strength. I love to praise and worship God, and it has brought me through many circumstances and situations. As the Christian phrase says, "Sometimes you have to worship your way through some things." Healing and deliverance can manifest through and during praise and worship unto God. These are just some examples of how the joy of the Lord can be your strength, Hallelujah.

The third Fruit of the Spirit listed in **Galatians 5** is peace. A good Scripture reference for peace, which is illustrated in the words of Jesus, comes from **John 14:27 (TPT)**: *"I leave the gift of peace with* *you—my peace. Not the kind of fragile peace given by the world, but my perfect peace. Don't yield to fear or be troubled in your hearts—instead, be courageous!"*

One of my favorite Scriptures about peace is **Philippians 4:6-7 (TPT)**, which says, *"Don't be pulled in different directions or worried about a thing. Be saturated in prayer throughout each day, offering your faith-filled requests before God with overflowing gratitude. Tell him every detail of your life, then God's wonderful peace that transcends human understanding, will guard your heart and mind through Jesus Christ."*

One thing regarding peace as a Fruit of the Spirit is that it will sustain you through any circumstance in your life. It is crucial to hold on to peace during the trials and tribulations of life. Furthermore, our peace comes from God because God is peace. As a matter of fact, one of the Redemptive Names of God is Jehovah-Shalom, which means "the Lord is peace." **Judges 6:24a (NLT)** acknowledges this name for God when it says, *"And Gideon built an altar to the Lord there and named it Yahweh-Shalom (which means 'the Lord is peace')."* In the context of **Judges 6:11-24**, an angel of the Lord came to the biblical character Gideon to encourage, comfort, strengthen, and give peace to him. The angel of the Lord called Gideon a mighty man of valor and then told Gideon to rescue Israel from the Midianites. However, Gideon was initially discouraged and had doubt, replying, *"How can I rescue Israel? My clan is the weakest in the whole tribe of Manasseh, and I am the least in my entire family!"* **(Judges 6:15b, NLT)**. Eventually, Gideon was encouraged to rescue Israel from the Midianites and began to have peace. Therefore, Gideon decided to build the altar to the Lord, naming it Jehovah-Shalom.

The fourth Fruit of the Spirit listed in **Galatians 5** is patience. A good Scripture reference about patience comes from **Romans 5:3-5 (TPT)**, which says, *"Even in times of trouble we have a joyful confidence, knowing that our pressures will develop in us patient endurance. And patient endurance will refine our character, and proven character leads us back to hope. And this hope is not a disappointing fantasy, because we can now experience the endless love of God cascading into our hearts through the Holy Spirit who lives in us!"*

Personally, I must admit that patience is one of the Fruits of the Spirit that I need to develop more. I confess that in certain situations, I can be impatient. For example, I can be impatient when driving, especially if I am in a hurry to get somewhere, and if I'm driving behind a slow driver or if traffic is slow. I can also be impatient while waiting in long lines. I confess that I don't even like waiting in a long checkout line at the grocery store. I am being transparent and honest about the lack of patience that I have at times; however, it is my responsibility to check myself when I find that I'm being impatient. One way that I deal with being impatient is that I pray to God to help me to be patient, and at the same time, I repent to God for my impatience. Also, I ask the Holy Spirit to help in me display patience. In addition, when I can, I may sometimes just start speaking in tongues while in the midst of being impatient. If we want to be pleasing in God's sight, that's exactly what we need to do: check ourselves when we fall short of God's glorious standards.

The fifth Fruit of the Spirit listed in **Galatians 5** is kindness. A Scripture reference regarding kindness is in **Ephesians 4:32a (TPT)**, which says, *"But instead be kind and affectionate toward one another. Has God graciously forgiven you? Then graciously forgive one another in the depths of Christ's love."* Another Scripture about kindness is

Proverbs 11:17 (TPT): *"A man of kindness attracts favor, while a cruel man attracts nothing but trouble."*

The Greek word for "kind" is *chrestos*, which means "to be serviceable." I have started an outreach ministry at my church called "Good Samaritans" Outreach Ministry, which does serviceable acts of kindness for the less fortunate and for those with severe needs. Over the years, our "Good Samaritans" Outreach Ministry has done serviceable acts of kindness such as Adopt-a-Family during the Christmas holiday, donating back-to-school items to an elementary school, and donating water and non-perishable foods to locations that had natural disasters. Personally, I want to testify that it's a blessing when you can show acts of kindness toward others.

The sixth Fruit of the Spirit listed in **Galatians 5** is goodness. One Scripture reference regarding goodness comes from **Galatians 6:9-10 (NLT)**, which says, *"So let's not get tired of doing what is good. At just the right time we will reap a harvest of blessing if we don't give up. Therefore, whenever we have the opportunity, we should do good to everyone—especially to those in the family of faith."*

There are many opportunities for each of us to be good to others. For example, just praying for others during their time of need is a form of being good to them. Being good to others helps them to feel blessed and encouraged. At this time, I would like to share a personal testimony about how a person blessed me by being good to me. Recently, I was at the grocery store in the checkout line. I was just about to pay for my groceries when another customer gave me a coupon that would take $5 off the cost. I was very appreciative and grateful.

Another Scripture reference regarding goodness comes from **Romans 12:9 (NLT)**, which says, *"Don't just pretend to love others. Really love them. Hate what is wrong. Hold tightly to what is good."*

Now I would like to share some testimonies of when I have chosen the opportunity to be good to others. I am a genuine, compassionate type of person. Many times, when I see homeless people on the streets, I give them money and a Bible tract, which I keep in my purse. In addition, sometimes I invite them to my church, and at times, I have asked them if they are saved. I will never forget the time some years ago when God used me to be good to a lady while I was at a restaurant. I encountered her outside in front of a Chinese restaurant, and she asked me for money. I knew that I was going to eat my lunch there, so I told the lady, "I am about to buy me a meal, and I already know that it's going to be more than enough for me, so how about I share this food with you?" The lady agreed for me to share the food with her. When I bought the food, I chose a table for both of us to sit at, and then I shared the food with her. During my conversation with her, I talked with her about job opportunities and some steps that may help her to find a job. The lady was very grateful and encouraged.

The seventh Fruit of the Spirit listed in **Galatians 5** is faithfulness. A good Scripture reference about faithfulness comes from **Proverbs 2:8 (NLT)**, which says, *"He guards the path of the just and protects those who are faithful to him."* Another one is **Psalm 37:29 (TPT)**, which says, *"The faithful lovers of God will inherit the earth and enjoy every promise of God's care, dwelling in peace forever."*

In addition, **Proverbs 28:20a (KJV)** says, *"A faithful man shall abound with blessings."* It is important for us to be faithful to God and to the assignment that God has given us.

The eighth Fruit of the Spirit listed in **Galatians 5** is gentleness. One good Scripture reference for gentleness is **Philippians 4:5 (TPT)**, which says, *"And let gentleness be seen in every relationship, for our Lord is ever near."* Another one is **Ephesians 4:1b-2 (TPT)**, which says, *"I plead with you to walk holy, in a way that is suitable to your high rank, given to you in your divine calling. With tender humility and quiet patience, always demonstrate gentleness and generous love toward one another, especially toward those who may try your patience."* In addition, **Matthew 5:5 (TPT)** says, *"What blessing comes to you when gentleness lives in you! For you will inherit the earth."*

The ninth and last Fruit of the Spirit listed in **Galatians 5** is self-control. One Scripture regarding self-control comes from **Proverbs 25:28 (NLT)**, which says, *"A person without self-control is like a city with broken-down walls."* Another one is **Proverbs 16:32 (NLT)**, which states, *"Better to be patient than powerful; better to have self-control than to conquer a city."* Also, **Titus 2:11-12 (TPT)** says, *"God's marvelous grace has manifested in person, bringing salvation for everyone. This same grace teaches us how to live each day as we turn our backs on ungodliness and indulgent lifestyles, and it equips us to live self-controlled, upright, godly lives in this present age."*

There are different areas of our life where we can display self-control. One way to display self-control is with our emotions. A Scripture illustration of this is in **James 1:19-20 (NLT)**, which says, *"Understand this, my dear brothers and sisters: You must all be quick to listen, slow to speak, and slow to get angry. Human anger does not produce the righteousness God desires."*

Another way that we can show self-control is with our eating habits. In **Matthew 6:25 (NLT)**, Jesus says, *"That is why I tell you not to* *worry about everyday life—whether you have enough food and drink, or enough clothes to wear. Isn't life more than food, and your body more than clothing?"* Additionally, He says in **Matthew 6:31-32 (NLT)**, *"So don't worry about these things, saying, 'What will we eat? What will we drink? What will we wear?' These things dominate the thoughts of unbelievers, but your heavenly Father already knows all your needs."*

It is also important to have self-control against sexual immorality. A good Scripture reference comes from **1 Corinthians 6:18-20 (NLT)**, which says, *"Run from sexual sin! No other sin so clearly affects the body as this one does. For sexual immorality is a sin against your own body. Don't you realize that your body is the temple of the Holy Spirit, who lives in you and was given to you by God? You do not belong to yourself, for God bought you with a high price. So you must honor God with your body."*

Prayer: God, please help us to bear good fruit in our lives with the leading and guidance of the Holy Spirit. Heavenly God, please help us to display all nine of the Fruits of the Spirit in our lives, which are love, joy, peace, patience, kindness, goodness, faithfulness, gentleness, and self-control. Yes, God, we want to be pleasing in your sight. Heavenly God, please continue your transforming work in our lives. In Jesus' Name, Amen.

Write Your Own Prayer

Chapter 5

IMITATORS OF JESUS

Our Lord and Savior Jesus Christ is the ultimate example for us Christians. While Jesus was on earth, He lived a perfect lifestyle unto God. Also, Jesus was obedient to God, even unto death. This is illustrated in the Scripture **Philippians 2:5-11 (NLT)**, which says, *"You must have the same attitude that Christ Jesus had. Though he was God, he did not think of equality with God as something to cling to. Instead, he gave up his divine privileges; he took the humble position of a slave and was born as a human being. When he appeared in human form, he humbled himself in obedience to God and died a criminal's death on a cross. Therefore, God elevated him to the place of highest honor and gave him the name above all other names, that at the name of Jesus every knee should bow, in heaven and on earth and under the earth, and every tongue declare that Jesus Christ is Lord, to the glory of God the Father."*

Prayer: Heavenly God, please help us to have the same mind that Christ Jesus had. Our Lord and Savior Jesus was very humble. God, please help us to be humble in spirit. Also, Jesus was always obedient to you, God. Yes, God, please help us to be obedient to you in all our ways. In Jesus' Name, Amen.

One way that Christians can imitate Jesus is by having a heart of compassion, just as Jesus did. One Scripture reference about Jesus having a heart of compassion is **Matthew 15:32 (NKJV)**, which says, *"Now Jesus called His disciples to Himself and said, 'I have compassion on the multitude, because they have now continued with Me three days and have nothing to eat. And I do not want to send them away hungry, lest they faint on the way.'"*

Jesus is also shown having compassion in **Matthew 9:35-36 (NKJV)**: *"Then Jesus went about all the cities and villages, teaching in their synagogues, preaching the gospel of the kingdom, and healing every sickness and every disease among the people. But when He saw the multitudes, He was moved with compassion for them, because they were weary and scattered, like sheep having no shepherd."*

Another Scripture about Jesus having compassion is **Matthew 14:14 (NLT)**, which says, *"Jesus saw the huge crowd as he stepped from the boat, and he had compassion on them and healed their sick."*

Jesus' heart of compassion is illustrated again in **Matthew 20:29-30 (NKJV)**: *"Now as they went out of Jericho, a great multitude followed Him. And behold, two blind men sitting by the road, when they heard that Jesus was passing by, cried out, saying, 'Have mercy on us, O Lord, Son of David!'"* **Matthew 20:34 (NKJV)** says, *"So Jesus had compassion and touched their eyes. And immediately their eyes received sight, and they followed Him."*

Prayer: God, I pray to you that you would help us to have a heart of compassion, just as Jesus did. Yes, God, let us be moved with compassion in our interactions with others, In Jesus' Name, Amen.

Another way we can imitate Jesus is by serving. Jesus teaches His disciples about serving others in the Scripture **Mark 10:42-45 (NLT)**: *"So Jesus called them together and said, 'You know that the rulers in this world lord it over their people, and officials flaunt their authority over those under them. But among you it will be different. Whoever wants to be a leader among you must be your servant, and whoever wants to be first among you must be the slave of everyone else. For even the Son of Man came not to be served but to serve others and to give his life as a ransom for many.'"*

Another Scripture that encourages us to serve is **Galatians 5:13 (NLT)**, which says, *"For you have been called to live in freedom, my brothers and sisters. But don't use your freedom to satisfy your sinful nature. Instead, use your freedom to serve one another in love."*

In **Luke 22:26b-27 (TPT)**, Jesus tells His disciples, *"You will lead by a different model. The greatest one among you will live as one called to serve others without honor. The greatest honor and authority is reserved for the one who has a servant heart. The leaders who are served are the most important in your eyes, but in the kingdom, it is the servants who lead. Am I not here with you as one who serves?"*

Jesus illustrated an example of serving to His disciples when He washed their feet. The Scripture reference comes from **John 13:4-5 (NLT)**, which says, *"So he got up from the table, took off his robe, wrapped a towel around his waist, and poured water into a basin. Then he began to wash the disciples' feet, drying them with the towel he had around him."* **John 13:12-15 (NLT)** continues, *"After washing their feet, he put on his robe again and sat down and asked, 'Do you understand what I was doing? You call me "Teacher" and "Lord," and you are right, because that's what I am. And since I, your Lord and Teacher,* *have washed your feet, you ought to wash each other's feet. I have given you an example to follow. Do as I have done to you.'"*

Prayer: Heavenly Father God, I ask that you teach us and help us to serve. Lord Jesus, you are the greatest example for us in learning how to serve, as you have demonstrated serving in the Scriptures. Yes, God, please help us to be good servants to you and to serve others. In Jesus' Name, Amen.

Another way to imitate Jesus is by showing love for others. Jesus demonstrated His love when He prayed in intercession for us believers. The Scripture reference is **John 17:20-23 (NLT)**, in which Jesus says, *"I am praying not only for these disciples but also for all who will ever believe in me through their message. I pray that they will all be one, just as you and I are one—as you are in me, Father, and I am in you. And may they be in us so that the world will believe you sent me. I have given them the glory you gave me, so they may be one as we are one. I am in them and you are in me. May they experience such perfect unity that the world will know that you sent me and that you love them as much as you love me."*

The love of Jesus is also shown in the Scripture **John 3:16 (NLT)**, in which He states, *"For God loved the world so much that he gave his one and only Son, so that everyone who believes in him will not perish but have eternal life."*

In addition, Jesus tells us exactly how much He loves us in **John 15:12-14 (NLT)**: *"This is my commandment: Love each other in the same way I have loved you. There is no greater love than to lay down one's life for one's friends. You are my friends if you do what I command."*

Furthermore, Jesus gave us an ultimate example of how to love our enemies and those who have offense toward us, when He prayed for those who crucified Him on the cross in **Luke 23:34a (NLT)**: *"Jesus said, 'Father, forgive them, for they don't know what they are doing.'"*

Can you imagine how Jesus was whipped and received 39 stripes? Jesus was beaten so badly to the point that He was unrecognizable. Then Jesus was nailed to a cross, and He bled out all His blood, and yet He still had the dignity to pray out of love for those who had crucified Him.

Prayer: Heavenly God, please help us to love just as you and Jesus love. Please help us to love others enough to intercede in prayer for them, just as Jesus interceded in prayer for us out of His love for us. God, please help us to also love our enemies and be willing to pray in intercession for them, just as Jesus prayed for those who had offense against Him. In Jesus' Name, Amen.

How many of you remember "What would Jesus do (WWJD)?" The WWJD theme was very inspirational, and it became a popular biblical theme. People began to wear WWJD clothes and jewelry to support it. Personally, I wore my WWJD pin with pride.

There are a number of Scriptures that illustrate that we should follow the example of Christ Jesus. One of them is **Ephesians 5:1-2a (NLT)**, which says, *"Imitate God, therefore, in everything you do, because you are his dear children. Live a life filled with love, following the example of Christ."* Similarly, **1 Corinthians 11:1 (NKJV)** says, *"Imitate me, just as I also imitate Christ."*

Write Your Own Prayer

Chapter 6

BEING A WITNESS FOR JESUS

As Christians, we are to be witnesses for Christ Jesus by sharing our faith with those who are not yet saved. I have a passion for sharing my faith with others. Through some training and from my Christian experience, I have learned how to be a witness for Christ Jesus.

There are different avenues to being a witness for Christ Jesus. One of them is to share your testimony about how you got saved with others. At this time, I want to share my salvation testimony.

My Personal Salvation Testimony

I didn't get saved until I was 19 years old. I thank God that during my childhood, I had a grandmother who had a strong faith in God, and who was able to sow seeds of faith into my life. When I was a child, my grandmother would teach me different Scriptures and give me suggested Scriptures to read. Also, it was my grandmother who taught me the "Jesus loves me, this I know" church song.

I did not grow up going to church much during my childhood. There were times when my family and I would visit some churches now and then, but we weren't members of any church, nor were we able to attend church regularly. However, I always knew that there was a

God because my grandmother often talked to me about Him. When I turned 19 years old, I was finally able to join a church and get saved.

During my life, I have been through and been able to overcome different circumstances and situations that many people don't even know about. However, I thank God that I don't look like what I have been through.

Since getting saved at the age of 19, I have discovered that everything that I need is through my faith in Jesus and my trust in Him as my Lord. I have also learned to trust and depend on the promises that God has for me in His written Word (the Bible).

Now that I have been saved for many years, I'm not saying that my life is perfect, but I can trust and depend on Jesus to be the solution to overcome any problem I may go through. I can honestly say that if it had not been for Jesus in my life, I don't know where I would be.

During the times in my life when I didn't have a job and income was low, Jesus provided for me and supplied all my needs. During the times when I needed encouragement, I held on to my faith in Jesus and His Word in **Philippians 4:13 (NKJV)**, which says, *"I can do all things through Christ who strengthens me."* During the times when I needed direction and guidance, I held on to the promise of Jesus in **Proverbs 3:5-6 (NKJV)**: *"Trust in the Lord with all your heart, and lean not on your own understanding. In all your ways acknowledge Him, and He shall direct your paths."* And this same Jesus can make a difference for the better in your life.

Another avenue to being a witness for Christ Jesus is to hand out Bible tracts to people who are not yet saved. Bible tracts usually explain the basics about being a Christian, and many have a salvation prayer to lead those who are not yet saved into salvation. Personally, I love using Bible tracts as an avenue for being a witness for Christ Jesus, especially to meet the spiritual needs of homeless people on the streets. If you give a Bible tract to a homeless person who is not already saved, you can lead them into a salvation prayer.

In addition, your lifestyle can be a witness for Christ Jesus. Christians should be willing to invite people who are not yet saved to their church services. In addition, as Christians, we can impart spiritual seeds into the lives of people who are not yet saved through Scriptures, prayers, discipleship, etc. Our lifestyle as Christians can be a witness for people around us who are not yet saved as we allow them to sense and feel the Jesus in us. In **2 Corinthians 5:20 (TPT)**, it says, *"We are ambassadors of the Anointed One who carry the message of Christ to the world, as though God were tenderly pleading with them directly through our lips. So we tenderly plead with you on Christ's behalf, 'Turn back to God and be reconciled to him.'"*

Salvation Is Available for Everyone

The Scripture **Romans 10:13 (NLT)** illustrates that salvation is available for everyone: *"For 'Everyone who calls on the name of the Lord will be saved.'"* In addition, **Acts 4:12 (TPT)** says, *"There is no one else who has the power to save us, for there is only one name to whom God has given authority by which we must experience salvation: the name of Jesus."* **Romans 10:17 (NLT)** says, *"So faith comes from hearing, that is, hearing the Good News about Christ."*

The Good News about Christ is that God sent His Son Jesus Christ into the world to save us from our sins and offer us His gift of salvation with the benefit of eternal life in heaven. We simply need to confess our sins to God. Then we need to acknowledge that Jesus died on the cross for our sins. We just need to invite Jesus into our heart and confess and allow Him to be Lord of our life.

For those of you who are not yet saved. I would like to offer you an invitation to accept Jesus into your heart for salvation so that you can begin to go through the process of fulfilling your God-given purpose in life. If you accept this invitation for salvation, then please say this salvation prayer.

Salvation Prayer: Lord Jesus, I admit that I need you as my Savior. Lord Jesus, I accept you into my heart for salvation. Lord Jesus, I want to develop a relationship with you. Lord Jesus, I want a fresh start with you. Lord Jesus, I commit myself to a life of following you, and I allow you to do a Transforming Work in me. And Lord Jesus, I am looking forward to fulfilling the God-given purpose that you have for my life. In your name, Jesus, I pray. Amen.

Amen, and I want you to know that if you have accepted this invitation to salvation, God has given you a fresh start today.

Write Your Own Prayer

_____

_____

_____

_____

_____

_____

_____

_____

_____

_____

_____

_____

_____

_____

_____

_____

_____

_____

_____

CONCLUSION

When Christians are authentically transformed, then they can sincerely be a bridge to help those who are unsaved unto salvation. Transformed Christians can be a witness for Jesus.

Christians are to be transformed away from who they used to be before they got saved. The Scripture **2 Corinthians 5:17 (NLT)** says, *"This means that anyone who belongs to Christ has become a new person. The old life is gone, a new life has begun!"*

Christians are to be led by the Holy Spirit. In **John 14:26 (NLT)**, Jesus says, *"But when the Father sends the Advocate as my representative—that is, the Holy Spirit—he will teach you everything and will remind you of everything I have told you."*

Finally, as Christians, we are to be a witness for Jesus by sharing our faith with those who are not yet saved. Even our lifestyle can be a witness for Jesus. People should be able to see and feel the love of Jesus in us.

At this time, I want to tell you about my journey from when I got saved up until the person I am as a Christian now. I got saved at a Baptist church in the year 1993. I was a member of that church for seven years, and when I first joined, I got baptized there and went through the new members classes. In addition, I was a faithful member of the church choir there.

In 2001, I joined an Equipping Ministry, where I learned how to speak in tongues and learned about the Fivefold Ministry Gifts of the Apostle, Prophet, Evangelist, Pastor, and Teacher. It is while I was in that Equipping Ministry that I first realized that I am called to evangelism.

I have been a member of Cincinnati Bible Way Church since 2003. When I first joined, I went through the new members class. My first ministry assignment at Cincinnati Bible Way Church was being an assistant Sunday school teacher for the nursery class for kids ages of three to five. Then I joined the Praise and Worship Team. In addition, I led the Health Ministry for seven years. For the past nine years, I have been the Ministry Leader over the Outreach Ministry.

In 2010, I went through the School of Ministry classes at my current church, which were for people who sense a Ministry Calling over their life. The church members who went through the School of Ministry graduated in 2013, and we all had the opportunity to receive our Ministry License. Personally, I was not going to rush to get my Ministry License; I wanted to take my time and realize for myself between me and God whether I was called to be a minister. Over the years, I started to become more and more aware of the anointing that I have over my life for the Word of God. For example, whenever I am praying for someone or even just offering encouragement to them, the Word of God just flows out of my mouth. I tend to speak forth Scriptures as I pray and encourage people. When I came to the realization of the anointing that I have on my life for the Word of God, I told my Pastors, and I received my Ministry License in 2017.

Currently, I have been doing sermons on Facebook Live. Sometimes I get amazed with how God uses me.

Readers, I encourage you to get a revelation from God regarding your spiritual gifts, anointings and purpose that God has called you to do for His Glory. May all those who are called to a Fivefold Ministry Gift of an Apostle, Prophet, Evangelist, Pastor, or Teacher rise up. May all those who are called to be an ordained or licensed minister rise up and preach and teach the Word of God. May all those who are called to serve in their church as Deacons rise up and serve their Pastors and the church. I encourage all of you, readers, to be all that God has called you to be for His Glory.

My prayer is that this book has inspired you and ministered to you. May this book continue to be an absolute blessing to you. May God abundantly bless you. Allow people to see and feel the Jesus in you. Finally, always be willing to share the Good News of the Gospel about Jesus Christ.

FIVE ADDITIONAL PRAYERS

Salvation Prayer (Prayer 1)

Lord Jesus, I accept the invitation for my salvation. Lord Jesus, I seek to know you. Jesus, I am grateful that you know me by name. Lord Jesus, I repent of my sins. Lord Jesus, I receive you into my heart. Lord Jesus, I choose to be obedient to your ways and your word. Lord Jesus, I ask you to be Lord over my life. I confess you, Jesus, as my Savior. In Jesus' Name, Amen.

Salvation Scriptures

Romans 10:13 (NLT): *"For 'Everyone who calls on the name of the Lord will be saved.'"*

Acts 4:12 (TPT): *"There is no one else who has the power to save us, for there is only one name to whom God has given authority by which we must experience salvation: the name of Jesus."*

Prayer to Find a Church Home (Prayer 2)

Heavenly God, I pray for all those people who are currently looking for a church home. God, please reveal to those people the church that you, God, want to place them in. Yes, God, please lead, guide, order their steps and direct their paths into the church that you would have them to be a member of. God, please lead those who are looking for a church into a good Bible-teaching, Holy Spirit-filled, Anointed church that will bring them into spiritual maturity. In Jesus' Name, Amen.

Scripture

Ephesians 4:5-6 (NLT): *"There is one Lord, one faith, one baptism, and one God and Father, who is over all and in all and living through all."*

Prayer for New Christians (Prayer 3)

Heavenly God, I intercede in prayer for all of those who recently got saved and/or are New Christians. God, please place them in a church or send people into their lives who will help disciple them. God, please help these New Christians to develop a relationship with you. God, I pray that you bring a spiritual understanding of the Scriptures of your Holy Bible to these New Christians with spiritual insight and revelations from you. Heavenly God, I pray that you begin the process of spiritual maturity for these New Christians. In Jesus' Name, Amen.

Scripture

2 Corinthians 5:17 (NLT): *"This means that anyone who belongs to Christ has become a new person. The old life is gone; a new life has begun!"*

Prayers to Fulfill Your God-Given Purpose, Calling, and Anointing (Prayer 4)

Heavenly God, you have an individual purpose for each of us. God, I pray that you reveal to us the God-Given Purpose, Calling and Anointing that you have placed on our lives. God, please help us to stay in our lane and not to compare ourselves or compete with others. God, please help us not to envy other people's gifts but to appreciate whom you have anointed, purposed, and called us to be. God, thank you for what the Scripture says in **Philippians 1:6 (NLT)**, that you, God, who began the good work within us, will continue your work until it is finally finished on the day when Christ Jesus returns. God, please help us to fulfill the purpose that you have for our lives. In Jesus' Name, Amen.

Scripture

Jeremiah 29:11 (NLT): *"For I know the plans I have for you," says the Lord. 'They are plans for good and not for disaster, to give you a future and a hope.'"*

Prayer to Be a Witness for Christ Jesus (Prayer 5)

Heavenly God, I pray that you give us the spiritual boldness to be witnesses for Christ Jesus. God, please teach us and reveal to us how to be a good witness for Christ Jesus to those who are not yet saved. Yes, God, please help us to share the Good News of the Gospel of Jesus Christ. Heavenly God, I pray that you will even let our lifestyle be a witness, so that people can discern and feel the Christ Jesus in us. God, please help us to be good representatives for Christ Jesus and empower us as witnesses for Christ Jesus. In Jesus' Name, Amen.

Scripture

1 Peter 3:15 (NLT): *"Instead, you must worship Christ as Lord of your life. And if someone asks about your Christian hope, always be ready to explain it."*

GLOSSARY OF BIBLE TRANSLATIONS

1) King James Version. Copyright 2010.
Holman Bible Publishers

2) New King James Version. Copyright 1991.
Thomas Nelson Publishers

3) The Passion Translation. 2020 Edition.
Broadstreet Publishing Group, LLC

4) Hebrew-Greek Key Word Study Bible (New King James Version).
Copyright 1984, 1990, 1991, 1996, 2013, and 2015.
AMG Publishers

5) New Living Translation. Copyright 2007.

BIBLIOGRAPHY

1) New Strong's Concise Concordance. Copyright 1997, 1999 by Thomas Nelson, Inc.

2) Vine's Concise Dictionary. Copyright 1997, 1999 by Thomas Nelson, Inc.

www.ingramcontent.com/pod-product-compliance
Lightning Source LLC
Chambersburg PA
CBHW071112090426
42737CB00013B/2577